SONS AND DAUGHTERS OF GAIA

BALANCING THE SEXES
TO BALANCE THE WORLD

ANGELA BAKER

Copyright © 2020, Angela Baker

All rights reserved. No part of this publication may be reproduced, distributed or transmitted in any form or by any means without permission of the publisher, except in the case of brief quotations referencing the body of work and in accordance with copyright law.

ISBN: 978-1-913479-27-5 (paperback)
ISBN: 978-1-913479-28-2 (ebook)

That Guy's House
20-22 Wenlock Road
London
England
N1 7GU
www.thatGuysHouse.com

The world is run by warmongers and
misogynists of both sexes.
Why?
That is the big question.
This book is about who you are,
what to ask yourself,
how to answer the big question
and change the world.

As with everything I do, this is a collaboration between me and my guides. I channel when I write. Ego, like the dog I no longer have, is left in the kitchen. Each chapter starts with a statement. Many are mine. Many are anonymous. If I have inadvertently taken one from a known source, I apologise.

The painting THE CHALICE AND THE BLADE, featured on the cover, was painted by me and the cover was designed by Peter John Bailey and his brother Anthony Bailey proofread and helped clarify the text.

CONTENTS

Chapter One: Human experiment 1

Chapter Two: Boarders and fences 5

Chapter Three: Surrendering power 11

Chapter Four: Stand alone together 15

Chapter Five: Here on a visit 19

Chapter Six: Nurturing the seed-corn 23

Chapter Seven: Seeking the balance 27

Chapter Eight: Women set aside 33

Chapter Nine: Standing up to fear 37

Chapter Ten: Question the norm 41

Chapter Eleven: We are all giants 45

Chapter Twelve: Empathy and love 49

Chapter Thirteen: Acknowledge your planet 53

Chapter One

*Sound came first. Musical vibrations create everything.
They are the source of life.*

IN Christian mythology, Eve was tempted by curiosity to eat the apple from the tree of knowledge and so brought trouble and pain into the world. I think it was more about enlightenment and learning. A long time has passed since then and we are still waiting for enlightenment's worldwide spread. That does not necessarily apply to those the West calls primitive people as they are often far more enlightened than the so-called civilised ones.
The message was the same in Greek mythology with a slightly different twist. Pandora was the first woman in the world and was sent by the gods as a punishment to Prometheus the demigod who was accused of stealing fire from the gods. The complaint against Pandora was that, through weak female curiosity, she opened the lid on her amphora and let all the troubles escape out into world.
    Curiosity is a word that is constantly used to criticise the natural search for knowledge. The search for knowledge as well as learning to love without judgement or ties are our prime reasons for incarnating into this dimension. The task is not an easy one but hand in hand with the difficult search for and

attainment of knowledge comes enlightenment, growth and love without fear or judgment.

The Christians thought that Eve was an afterthought and an aid to Adam. What an extraordinary idea. One could be rather rude and say perhaps she was here to be an improvement on the prototype but very early historical myths might be excused from such wild claims. Remember, they were and still are just myths.

Our first figures of worship were the female goddesses of human fecundity and earth's fertility. Along with the water goddess, they were universal, prayed to and given offerings of thanks. They protected the home and balanced the seasons and the world of nature. All things that we regard as animate or inanimate including the planet have a powerful intelligence. The intelligence of Gaia is the most powerful. We are just a small cog in the wheel.

After the start with the female goddesses, along came the male gods. They brought the rules and the start of a rather judgmental society. They appear to be rather bad-tempered and punishing most of the time. With the commencement of organised religion, it all looks a bit like control and rule.

All humans are born in this world with a strong sense of right and wrong although it does not always look it. The light is always far more powerful than the dark but the dark is more enticing and gets more publicity. The dark is fear. The light is not so tempting or easy but is far more rewarding.

Women have been systematically written out of history for a very long time. We have almost forgotten that they held an equal place with men in the earliest societies. On researching the accounts of many of the world's cultures, it is clear that women have been removed from written history, religion, painting, sculpture, music and science—the list goes on.

Women have been either defaced or unacknowledged or hidden by the predominately male interpretation of history. Women have often hidden behind a pseudonym or their husband's name, for this was a culture imposed upon us by the dominating section of society and that was male.

Only when humanity has balanced out the combination of both the male and the female energy contained equally in both sexes will the earth balance. Remember the profound message from the past, *'as above so below'*. All things need to be in a synergistic balance to harmonise both with us and the world. It's all about balance.

My guides are with me at all times and have told me not to be so cross with females who allowed themselves to be dominated if that was the norm in their time. I have a bit of a problem with this, having come from a line of strong-minded, liberated working women and having the powerful feminist planet Eris in a prominent position in my birth chart.

I am human so I must remember not to pass judgement but I do feel that all humans, whatever their sex, need to fulfil themselves and stretch themselves to their furthest boundaries. It is on planet earth that we can develop. It's not comfortable. In fact, it is often a very hard and lonely track. Many of us have forgotten why we came here.

Much information coming forward at this time has been found in many old records concerning the ancient equality between the sexes and their functions in the government and early belief systems in many parts of the world. Some information was hidden purposely and some semi-destroyed. Faces were changed or scrubbed out in wall paintings or ancient church paintings.

As well as obliterating records of female leaders, many were defamed or belittled. Heads were smashed off sculptures. Written histories of powerful females carved in stone were defaced. Records were broken, destroyed or buried.

It's all a bit like simple-minded, obsessional, male graffiti on advertising posters that are depicting females. It's as if one sex has gone around the world with a big rubber removing the other sex. It all smells of fear. In the latter part of the twentieth century and the start of the twenty-first, many female historians and archaeologists have been making it their duty, thank goodness, to uncover and reinstate the women to their equal and rightful place in world history.

Originally, humanity by its very physical nature was predominately a matriarchal society. Men were the hunters and women brought children into the world. They nurtured them. Care for the sick and the old fell to the women. They gathered the food. They were the guardians of the fire. Given their nomadic existence, they carried this fire from place to place. By gathering the food, they discovered and used medicinal plants because they were the main healers as well as the cooks. The women lived in close mutual support groups and the men went to hunt.

Life was ruled by the cycle of the moon. The men needed its light when they were hunting at night to know how far from the camp they were and how and when to return. There is still controversy about whether the women's fertility cycle synchronised with the moon and with each other's as often happens with certain animals. That way, they might become pregnant when the men returned. Life was all about procreation and nature is efficient.

Women were important instigators in the development of society because communication and the support of each other was to their mutual advantage. The majority of women to this day automatically cooperate, support and look out for each other. Cooperating and helping each other rather than competing is to our advantage and the best way to raise our children as it saves both resources and time.

The female does not have the defensive physical power of the male that suits men for close combat. The male has very different skills from the female. He is tenacious and far more resilient. Men as well as women have an intuitive sense and are natural detectives. *'Female intuition'* was a defence skill that came from observing and feeling into people and their thoughts from a great distance. That way, they felt their predator's intention. It gave them the advantage of moving before the danger was near. They were pregnant almost all the time so they had babies to care for as well as the old, sick and any animals that they had domesticated. The female still has this powerful intuition.

Men and women often had different roles in early society but we were working in unison for our survival. Neither sex was of greater superiority or value. Women were revered as the bringers of life into the world and that was very important at that time. All that mattered was fertility.

Chapter Two

The earth is moving now to make us care for her.
We and the earth are joined.
If she goes, we go.

ONE only has to view a pack of animals hunting to see how well cooperation works to the advantage of all. The rise of a world monopolised by the doubtful more male competitive inclination wastes resources as well as energy.

The development of permanently sited agricultural communities made a big difference to us and to the future of the planet. It was then that humans thought that they could own land. This attitude meant that there was something to guard, i.e. land, food and property.

There is a big difference between defence of one's own property and attack on other people's. This change was to be the start of borders and fear of others. Before this time, we all wandered at will across the planet The only borders in the natural world are sea, rivers and mountains. Animals, fish and birds have no conception of borders. If you look at a map of the world we have drawn, you will see strange straight lines through everything including mountain, river sea. It's illogical but oh so human.

The continual rise of the competitive males who are now joined by many females from the same mould are dinosaurs and will disappear unless they evolve. They are a waste of the planet's resources. All things now can only survive if they are conserved to improve life for all things on planet earth.

We must be grateful for the gradual change in education and rise of more flexible and balanced males and females in our midst. We should do all we can to encourage them and hope that they continue to step forward and become proud examples to the next generation of children both girls and boys. Both are equal in value. For many centuries, the female has been put down and now we see the devastating result of this imbalance.

Do not get me wrong. Just because I am female this is not a harangue against men. I love men and have a deep respect and compassion for them as well as women. Also, I had the experience of a very long marriage to one man and of spending a long working life closely associated with very many different men. The greater part of my working life was spent working one to one with men. Odd, I suppose, but I hardly ever worked with women.

This experience has led me to feel so sad about the innate vulnerability men have that keeps them closed tight for their protection. Our culture of *'man up'* has done that to them since they were small boys. Women as well as men have made them what they are now and we constantly reinforce this pattern of treatment. At last the tide is turning and many men are opening up to who they really are as Source intended: wonderful, fully rounded humans. It was and is society that distorted them.

Have we considered what type of human beings we have developed into and do we deserve planet earth? There have been many that have come and gone that have dedicated their lives to the good of humanity and the planet but the majority can't give a damn or think, *'I can't be arsed. It's the authorities' problem'*. It's not. It affects all, if not this time then the next time they are around and that won't be long.

Things are changing even though rather slowly. Hold on and who knows we might just start tearing the borders down between the people of the world, *'the other people, them over there'*. They are all us. We are all joined. We are one.

Animals and birds don't recognise borders so why do we? It makes life very wasteful on every front imaginable, especially as far as the world's resources, preservation and development are concerned. Don't say it's always been like that. We were the ones that made it so and we can change it.

The inhabitants of earth are very violent. Some of this violent energy has had its uses. It gave us the drive to produce forward momentum and was the force behind the eventual superiority of homo sapiens. It is also that drive that has sent the world out of balance. We have few predators other than each other.

We have self-determination in our planet's eventual outcome by what we put in and what we get out. Our capacity for warlike destruction is getting out of control and this is the constant threat that stops our progress towards manifesting a peaceful and productive world, a world that will align with both the physical and spiritual development of all.

Animate or what we consider inanimate, there is nothing in this world to which we cannot connect or communicate with. Nothing is surplus to the balance. The law of attraction is the most powerful energy you will ever experience. It has an abundance that is never-ending. It can only give and never judge what or who is worthy. Judgment is what we do all the time. The law of attraction is just a simple way of giving energy without judgment. The sun shines on the good and the bad. It's what we do with it that counts.

If you only see and put forward the thought that it never comes your way, that is what you will receive because you put the intentional thought out for it. If you show gratitude for all the abundance that comes your way and expect it, there will be more and more. The law of attraction never runs out.

Start afresh and look into your life. Look at all you are gifted with. Look at all the good that comes in, however small. Abundance comes in all shapes and sizes and not just through money. It might be good energy. It might be love. There is nothing in this universe that is without a meaning or purpose. It's up to us to face the direction of what we desire to be in our lives. Every person or thing or trial that comes into our life is here to teach us something and it is hardly ever seen in the moment but will be in retrospect.

The general rape of the planet's resources, greed and lack of forward planning for its regeneration is with us each day.

As well as the gross waste of fossil fuel there is the ongoing effect of irresponsible destruction of habitats and tree felling for plantations of one thing or another and all the rest of the get rich quick agri-business. I don't think the plantation owners give Gaia thanks each day. They give thanks to the chemical giants and overlook the slave labour they use. The cheap supermarket food depends on slaves in Europe now in the 21st century, all for the great god: Money.

Agricultural attitudes in general and irresponsible dosing of the planet with chemicals have contributed to the disastrous situation at this time. The rice and grain fields as well as the massive plantations that encroach upon the forests in many parts of the world are ruining the ecological balance by their massive size. They come with an arrogant disregard for the humans, animals, birds, insects and soil micro-organisms that dwelt there and are needed to keep the whole planet in balance. At this time, half the food produced is thrown away as waste. Add to this the irresponsible use of water needed for the crops that we grow in unsuitable places.

Consider the bizarre habit of growing lawns that are watered each week and mown each week. Grass is a graceful plant with beautiful flowers and seed heads but it is repeatedly mown down to resemble a carpet so strange. Question when we started doing it and whether we need to continue. Just because it was done when you were born does not mean it still has to be done. I wonder if grass is ever really thought of as a plant in its own right. Get down on the floor and look at it. In fact, stop a while each day and look at all things and start thinking what type of stewards of the planet we are.

All this greed compounds the damage to our mutual environment in the mad scramble to go forward but forward to what? There will be nowhere and nothing to go forward to.

Vegans and vegetarians must shoulder part of the responsibility for dumping the blame on the meat-eaters, which has become fashionable nowadays. Grain was not originally a primary food for homo sapiens as it is now. Our daily eating of grain, including our recent habit of eating cereal for breakfast that came about in the late nineteenth century, results in grain cultivation covering a huge part of the planet and strips the land that was manured by animals. Grain is not even very good for us. It turns into sugar and causes obesity in humans and animals. Learn to question all things we are subliminally brainwashed to believe.

We started as omnivores and were in constant migration, treading on the planet lightly. Growing grain takes its toll and causes irreversible damage, with exposed earth blowing away and leaving bare earth. This is not natural. There is no empty earth or a vacuum in nature. The more natural management of land by rotation of both crops and livestock is a more sensible and humane way to go forward. This way means the earth can grow, rest and fertilise naturally.

Our bodies are omnivores even if we think we aren't. Our body belongs to planet earth; we don't. Try to align with what it and the earth needs whilst you are its steward. In any situation of doubt, see when left to its own devices what nature does. It will tell you. Look at the wild places.

Chapter Three

I am provided with all I desire and need if I just trust and love with abundance.

ONE has only to consider the world situation as it is now to clearly see how more of the same in the future is a disaster. It is no good repeating something time and time again. If it did not improve things in the past, it won't in the future. It's not to our advantage to persist. Two wrongs have and will never make a right.

We do have a big problem at this time as instant profit appears to be the only thing that matters. The world's and our children's future must be our priority, as our planet is in an extremely pivotal condition on all fronts. There will be no future soon. We will tip over the safety line of automatic recovery.

It makes me happy that Gaia is far more powerful than us. It has its own intelligence and ways of balancing. When it has had enough, we will just be jettisoned. It has happened a number of times before. Thank goodness that it's just ego that tells us we are the most intelligent beings around here.

If you consider that the average human can hardly organise their own home and life, how can they keep the planet safe? I am glad that the planet has far greater intelligence than human beings.

Think about it. What will you have left to be reincarnated into? It will be a bit of a challenge next time, so how about making improvements now for our next sojourn on planet earth as well as our grand-children's current one.

Take the blinkers off. Stand up and say, '*No more*'. You are far greater and more powerful than you can ever imagine.

The major governments would be better looking after their own internal affairs and desist from ganging up behind the scenes to develop wars that make fortunes from the sale of arms to countries that would benefit from peace and real help with their development and prosperity.

The worldwide refugee problem has arisen from a complex mix of debt, war and famine, the latter usually compounded by disruption of a country's natural supply of resources. Films on the television and articles in the newspapers encourage us to give aid money for all those injured and displaced by war but it is our governments and manufacturers that make big money from the arms that continue these wars.

There would be no refugees if we did not do our best to destabilise other countries and then demand massive repayment from debts that they did not want. What they need is to help to develop and be independent and not to be the pawns of the bizarrely called '*civilised West*' that encourages them to buy more armaments to protect their country when they have nothing left to protect.

The time has come for us to realise that the world is just one planet with no separate borders or countries. Everything is alive, interconnected and self-perpetuating, including the planet. If we don't respect it now and realise that its bounty is not infinite, if we continue doing two wrongs to try to make a right, the planet will shake us off its back as a wet dog deals with water. It's done it before, a number of times. The planet can exist without us but we cannot exist without the planet.

Greed rules those that we vote into power to rule the planet. They will not be able to take their personal wealth and power with them when they go and the clock is rapidly counting down now. Not one of the power-mad countries stand up to really defend the planet without self-interest. They don't have anybody brave enough. All of them just do a bit of fiddling about. They just go through the motions because they are blinded by personal greed and are willing to destroy the future of generations to come.

This problem derives from the beliefs of many that we are not going to be the generation to come and this life is the only one we have. They will get an uncomfortable surprise when their time is up and cryogenics will be of no help. They will in common with all humans be back time and time and time again. That's what life is.

The majority of humanity is kept in a state of fear and neediness. The world has resources for everyone. There is more than enough space to support the world population and enable it to be fed. The people of this planet have the opportunity and the intelligence if the will is there to enable us. We have the brains and current technological abilities. It is possible for it to be a wonderful place that is able to support all.

Alas, now it's rushing headlong to total destruction. This has happened before a few times. It's not a myth. Take the blinkers off. We can't hide by looking the other way. We are not ostriches.

It's extraordinary that scientists discuss the probability of putting humans in to a state of dormancy so as to rocket them for a journey of probably twenty years or so to the next suitable planet that humans can perhaps survive on when this one is no longer viable. It's outrageous. Those that think and plan such things would be better occupied sorting out the mess they are making here first. It's rather like living in a house and moving into a different room when the present one is trashed. It's adolescent behaviour and we all know who will be the ones moving on, those with the power and money.

We are still far too underdeveloped to comprehend how the residents of our local universes travel about. They use the portals and energy streams between the planetary systems and dimensions, not fuel as we think we need. Humans are still stuck with knowledge that is far too primitive to get anywhere in a hurry thank goodness and, no, there are not strange creatures coming to attack us. That's fear again. The majority of other civilisations are far more advanced and interconnected.

Until we have advanced and developed a little respect and care for our inhabitants as well as our mother planet, we are sidelined. The information we desire to move on will come in at the right time through the right people.

On this planet, we have always had guardians watching over us. It was developed as a dualist planet and we are here to experience it and see what we can achieve. We receive the seeds of new ideas from time to time. They are sent as inspiration. Where do you think AI - *'artificial intelligence'* - comes from? Try looking at it as something dropped in our playpen.

As we are a dualist planet with borders, it's up to us what we do with it. We have a choice. Will we use it to get us out of our greedy, potentially disastrous, ecological mess and to improve life for all things living on this planet? Or to make it worse? It's all about how we use what we are given. That is the most important lesson. We are an experiment in duality and love.

I went through to my guides one day asking how we will combine AI and our spirituality. They had a quick answer for that one. AI came from Source to see what we can do with it and whether we use it for the dark or the light. Well, that was to the point and so obvious. As we reside on a dualist planet, it's up to us.

From time to time, someone incarnates with an idea and we often accuse them of being mad but, no, they are often just a bit advanced. Look back at the big steps taken in life and how they came about. It's how we use an idea that is important. We are all an experiment.

Chapter Four

We create all the suffering in this dimension.
We have created this world by our thoughts and actions.

OUR arrogant, warlike and destructive energies have given this planet a very energetically low, dense and troubled energy. I personally find it very hard here. All my life I have imagined myself as a diver in very deep muddy water, my suit heavy with air-pipes up to a small boat full of my helpers high above. I ask to come up from time to time but the answer is always the same: *'Hang on a bit longer. Remember what you came to do'*.

I have no religion and never have never had. The only thing I have is an absolute faith in a clear and direct connection with Source. I always have had. There is no need of a human interceding for me. I am what is referred to as a *claircognizant*. This is a metaphysical and psychic ability. There are many of us in this world. We are everywhere but we don't use our ability often, through fear or ridicule. We know, feel and hear within us not through our ears. The information comes through and is instant.

When working, I am physically surrounded by the energies that are here with me and always have been. They touch and pat me. I feel them bumping against me with excitement. They are here to help and guide me. When I am with them, there is no room or need for doubt or ego - just love and fun. They make me smile. Thank goodness that my connection with my guides and helpers is very powerful and clear. They are with me all day and all night.

Vibrationally sensitive humans have always had a hard time staying here but this is just one of the reasons why those humans, however sensitive, are also the very ones that this place needs to remain here as a conduit for the light. We can never bring too much light to balance the sadness, war, greed, destruction and darkness that surrounds us.

It is necessary to keep our eyes on the positive outcome of what could still be. It's never too late and never a time to give up on planet earth, however dim our light may be now. We are all potentially beings of light and all of us have the ability to do our bit to bring this place of such rich beauty, love and abundance into a harmonious balance.

From what you have read so far, you might imagine that I am a pessimist: by no means, just saddened by those wonderful people with so much going for them who are so unaware of the reality of our sick world. We are surrounded by those who never stand up but hide in the group and think, *'It's not my responsibility'* or *'I just want some fun'* or *'My debts are too big'*, or, the best one, *'We only live once'*. No. We will all be back here fast enough to a seriously not-much-fun world. Each one of us is the master of our world now and to come.

History shows us that the arrival of homo sapiens on this planet turned out to be very destructive. We are an experiment and have free will. This, in retrospect, is looking rather worrying. Those that guide and guard us hold back from interfering. Our freedom has given us the power to contribute to the energy that is pushing the planet out of its synergistic balance, so let us hope we have the will and determination to reverse this trend.

We have very little time left before we bring about our own as well as our world's destruction. Never forget the truth in the statement that big results start from many small actions. Take your own small actions. Don't wait until you have time.

The natural world knows how to balance itself. Nothing before our arrival has been as rampant as homo sapiens. Nature works to keep all things in check be they plant or animal. With our powerful brain, organisational ability and so few predators we are causing the total imbalance of all on the earth.

Each time we remove an animal, bird, fish or insect from our environment it changes nature's control of the whole system of balance. Each living thing depends on another. It all came together over thousands of years. If we remove a particular insect or predator from an area, something will take over that previously was kept under control. It will and does recover when we reinstate whatever we removed. We must not meddle with nature but learn from it.

We brought the seeds of our own destruction with us on the path of our development towards so-called civilisation. Now that's a big word and a very doubtful term. What does it really mean? Conquering various parts of the primitive world as it is normally described to bring about civilisation? Think about it. This is normally undertaken by the use of sword or gun or in present times far worse.

All comes under the heading of saving and enlightening those that we consider to be our inferiors by bestowing civilisation upon them. Conquering countries do not normally have benign intentions. They are just plunderers. Aggressive predatory civilisations have always thought that killing and stealing was what they needed to do to enable them to impose their point of view on others. So far, they have neither proved to be as successful or as civilised as the word might convey.

We have no right to impose our view or avaricious lifestyle on another. It would be far better to go with love and a sense of enquiry, observing how the so-called backward people live and what insights they can help us with.

What has the civilised West really got to offer other than a mobile phone or computer? Even these are but distractions and fear-bringers. They sap our prime energy and sense of direction. We are now overloaded with conflicting information and are being swept along in confusion. The mass of humanity is being led in circles by the nose. People have lost touch with their gut feeling, unable to discriminate between truth and lies, right and wrong.

Civilised medicine has brought progress in many areas but the baby has been thrown out with the bathwater. We must not lose our ability to heal ourselves with all the pure energy systems and herbal treatments from plants in many forms from around the world. They are still the best way to go at illness when combined with physical body work but these plants are being stolen every day with the intention of owning and licensing them by the big conglomerates. How can natural plant medicine be licensed and its use forbidden when it was given to us to use?

The bodies we inhabit are vehicles we use temporarily in this dimension to enable us with the development of our soul. So far, it's clear that when we are in our bodies we don't often listen to our greater selves. We drive around these vehicles as deaf, blind and lost. We are like road hogs most of the time. That all sounds a bit scary but on our arrival in this planet we have a grand loss of memory, a clean slate, a tabula rasa or so we hope so. It's rather disconcerting for those of us who don't.

The residents of planet earth might well all be described as drop-ins, with the temporary loan of a body. My guides usually refer to these as our vehicles and they are always telling me with amusement to look after mine. Having been trained as a herbalist and healer, I have the unfortunate habit of always looking after others and forgetting myself.

We are on a journey and in this world we experience life in one of the many dimensions that we inhabit.

Our different lives might not all be experienced in this world, nor all as humans as we recognise that state to be. I have existed in other places and other vehicles. I certainly have not always been incarnated as a human. Remember that we are not our body. We come to experience life from our higher self. Our body differs each time as we inherit tendencies from the genetic family we choose and its history before we arrive here. When we pass, we return to our soul family.

We have an earthly memory of timetables, riding a bike, phone numbers and so on but we also have a higher self memory of past lives and skills. People we related closely to in past lives can turn up again in our present life. Profound trauma from a past life can be triggered for some of us. The wall between different lives can be almost invisible and too much information can often be extremely painful.

Chapter Five

Your body is the vehicle for this dimension. Respect and care for it but do not confuse your mind with your body.

CAN you imagine what would happen if information were in the public domain that many of us on this planet at this crucial time are not from here but are only on a visit to help tip the scales at planet earth's crucial time? Can you imagine the reaction from the press and the rabble-roused crowds? They would be baying and slavering. It would be yet another witch hunt. Yes, I've been the prey in some of those. I was told that I will be safe this time. Most of us have been persecuted in some life or another.

This world usually has rabble-rousers going on about something or another - race, colour, religion or sexual preference. How humanity just loves them!

Volunteers from other dimensions incarnate on this planet in human form. At this time there are many thousands. They have come to help with the huge dimensional shift we are in the process of achieving over the next few generations.

Each human incarnation is a small spark, split from our higher self that itself is a spark from the great and benign energy of creation. None of these separate sparks splitting off diminishes the higher Source that wishes to experience life in all its forms and circumstances, however elevated, lowly or painful. The desire is to experience the whole spectrum. Nothing is exempted. Be careful not to judge.

It is difficult for us whilst residing in human form to comprehend how limitless and powerful our higher self is and also that we always have instant access to both its power and knowledge. The reason behind all life is to gain knowledge and this knowledge comes from all of our experiences in every dimension. With each life we develop from the experience of another previous or concurrent one.

The idea of karma as punishment is all part of the dualism belief. We do have a form of making a karmic contract with a person we have known from another life. We contract to help often after a previous traumatic relationship with them. Our aim is to finish our contracts. We all have or had karma to sort out. It's tying up loose ends. It is not bad luck. A lot can be put off. There are plenty of other times and lives but it is nice to sort it out so both sides of the contract can move on.

The thoughts and intentions of humans are very powerful so what we want to see and experience we do. Source lets the sun shine and the rain fall on all equally. It is not for us to judge. If we hate, it reflects back onto us causing negativity and unhappiness. If we love, it is water on a dry plant and all about us flourishes. We make our reality. When we step forward into our true selves and remove our minds from the straitjackets of fear that we have tucked them into for safety, we can expand and flower. Who knows what fruit we can bring to this world? Only fear stops us.

Our conception of time only exists on this planet, making it hard for earth-based humans to conceive that we are in many places at once. At least half the people on planet earth sleepwalk through life without ever raising an enquiring thought. There again, it's not for me to judge. Perhaps they wanted it that way this time or perhaps they are far too fearful of enquiring and poking everything with questions. *'Why? How?'* Sorry but I never get out of that age.

However diligent we are, we can never find enough answers to satisfy the ever-expanding quest. Our abilities are underused. Many people are unaware that our body is our vehicle in this dimension but it is not who we are. We are not a body. We are a constantly developing soul on an experience and learning trip. Who knows what leaps and bounds forward we will make over the next few thousand years? Let us hope that our vehicles are around and we still have a planet long enough to return in human form.

The most important thought to hold on to is that we are totally loved in a way that we find hard to conceive. Turning our back and denying this is the same as turning our back on the sun. We may not see it but its energy is still there and it's impossible to cut ourselves off from that truth as it also is with Source. The fact that you don't feel or believe it is irrelevant.

There is no person or circumstance that comes into our life by accident. All major situations and changes of direction are very often stimulated by serendipitous meetings or perhaps a chance remark from one who passes in what appears to be just a fleeting encounter. The time of arrival and their remark was possibly by prior arrangement. The encounter was to be a trigger to be acted on or ignored.

In our lives, there are many pre-arranged directional trigger points and portal exit points. It is our decision as to what we do about them, whether to take up an opportunity or pass on by.

Each life has many walk-on parts but the nucleus is peopled by those who we have a karmic link with. We incarnate together time after time. We turn and turn about, each taking a different relationship role. We are here to teach and learn through our relationships with each other.

Often it is to our advantage to feel or recognise one from a past encounter but there are also times that prior knowledge of them would inhibit or hinder our development. They might have loved us very much or they might have murdered us and vice-versa. To hold that knowledge is not comfortable, especially the latter.

Not all of us in this world at this time originate from it. Many have arrived from other worlds and dimensions. All are here to experience life here.

They have answered the call to bring in positive energy, love, empathy and compassion.

Many of these energies have never incarnated as a human before. This is not an easy transition for beings from other dimensions as the energy of this planet is dense, fearful and aggressive. All of this creates turbulent emotion and gives new arrivals stress with the fearful ego interaction and the subtle nuances of relationships and emotions.

Depression and suicide take many at an early age. Suicide is not a thing to take lightly as we ask to come here when we planned our task. Planet earth might be one of the most beautiful planets but it is also one of the densest as far as fear and emotional energy goes. It's not easy.

The suicide rate for the under thirties is a judgement on the state of the world that we have made for them. It is dreadful and something that we all should be very aware of. It is higher now than it has ever been in our history.

The suicide rate for young men is three times that of females. All too often, young males are unable to communicate their distress, surrounded as they are by constant reinforcement of negative male behaviour. They do not have a culture of mutual male bonding or support in the same way that females have built over many millennia.

Chapter Six

Strength is not needed to walk forward with truth and clarity but courage is important to enable us to drop our guard.

THE young of both sexes are urgently in need of powerful examples of love and fearlessness to look up to. They don't need warmongering brainless hulks or their partners, super-skinny shopping ninnies. Neither of these lost and pitiful extreme depictions of humanity, put forward by society for our desire, are the powerful life-affirming examples to identify with or follow.

In the past, older people were revered as the repository of the knowledge and wisdom of the clan. Now, they are sidelined. They have no monetary value so the majority of society regard them as having no value for the future generations. We all need deep roots of passed-down wisdom. That comes from the experience of living. It's no good saying that life is different now. In reality, only the outward appearance alters. Humans never do.

Many of the hyper and disruptive children of today go on to develop into adults that are clever loners, often classed as dyslexic or with Asperger syndrome. These are only labels and recent ones at that. Where would the world be without their input? Certainly it would have taken longer for computers, mobile phones or the internet for starters. Houston invites them in because of the type of brain they have. It has no walls around it. They are problem solvers. They have to try harder.

The system of standard education must learn to accommodate such children, realising that intelligence is not all of the same kind and that we cannot all be crammed into the same slot. These children are gifted in many ways and often have higher than average intelligence. When such recognition comes about, they will be appreciated as they always *'think outside the box'*. I asked to be born one. I'm proud of it. It's my gift.

There is an adage that applies to these children. It is very true and it was written by Albert Einstein, himself one of the many brilliant dyslexics:

> **'Everybody is a genius but if you judge a fish by its ability to climb a tree, it will live its whole life believing that it is stupid'.**

There is really no such thing as the norm, thank goodness. Many can be squeezed into it but many don't fit.

The veil that has in the past cut us off from our true self-knowledge, the barrier between us and our spiritual Source, is thinning rapidly. Total connectedness to all things as well as the multi-dimensional information concerning our existence is awakening the knowledge that we all have in us, though buried very deep in some that wish to remain in denial. That's OK. It's what they chose to do at this time.

Try to remember yourself as a young child and how very young children under the age of five develop. They take everything onboard, accept it and discuss things with no self-restrictions. They talk of friends and places and concepts that we cannot see or hear. Is theirs the place of fantasy or is ours?

As we develop and fully inhabit this dimension, we become cut off from our personal history, reality and the full knowledge of who we are. We are told, *'Don't be silly. That's not true'*, as we are fitted into the current accepted-belief straitjacket and blinkers. The majority of the population appear to exist in a world where they have worn glasses since childhood that have cut them off from half of what is out there and clear vision has become obscured.

We have come a long way in the last twenty years but many still are governed by fear. This is the strongest emotion that we humans feel other than love. Fear is inclined to limit our thinking as well as our actions. Fan the flames of fear and it causes a reaction. To react is to act out the same response as before so, with each new thing that comes in, learn to respond afresh without prior judgment. Act from your personal history reality and the full knowledge of who we are and were before we were fitted into what is the current accepted-belief straitjacket.

Humans start to restrict and blinker themselves by scaling down to what they wish to take in that will conform and be safe with their taught and prejudged view of what should and shouldn't be. Is it our old friend/enemy ego again trying to keep us safe? Ego belongs to the earth and is just to protect us. Make your own judgements. Release fear.

This self-imposed restriction limits us to half of what is really in front of our eyes, ears and our instinctive gut feelings. We repress so much because of fear of the unknown.

The rapid fear response that developed within us long ago was a response to being attacked by large savage animals. We react fast from experience so, in the future when you are confronted by new and challenging thoughts, take the time to feel safe. It's not a tiger. Consider all things from all sides. Question everything that comes up before responding.

It's not easy. We have to think really so hard sometimes that it physically hurts and it takes time to really think. Don't be in such a hurry to judge and rush on. You never know what you might discover about both yourself and the world about you when you stop to consider things before you act on something that is not a tiger or its equivalent.

Open up. Listen to your guides' advice. They are always with you. Ask them when in doubt. If time is taken to patiently work via meditation with progressively opening the higher chakras one by one in the right sequence and at the right time, one gently passes through the earthly brain of protective ego, enabling us to access the higher planes of all knowledge. It is on our higher planes we meet up with our higher self, our guides and helpers.

In the mid-twentieth century, psychiatrists and doctors started to walk into our oh so sensitive and highly balanced brains. As usual, they had lead boots on. They had the answer to everything so were experimenting with hallucinogenic as well as mood-altering drugs, brain surgery and electric shock treatment. All of these things are far too crude for the delicate balance of us humans. We are sensitive spiritual beings on a visit in this oh so heavy dimension.

These unthinkingly brutal treatments were to cause the higher chakras often to be torn open prematurely, leaving those sensitive souls with a long-term legacy of damage and confusion, resulting in multi-dimensional slippage. Many have suffered extreme reactions and have been left as shells by the experiments that they were subjected to, either by the overconfident caring professions or their own ignorance concerning the long-term reactions to any drugs that interfere with the brain function.

Experimentation with anything that interferes with the brain is rather foolhardy as most are in total ignorance and do not realise how we are extraordinarily, miraculously and delicately balanced beings consisting of numerous interwoven layers of the physical and spiritual body as well as our multi-dimension existences. Time spent in deep hypnosis regression work, raising and sorting out problems left over from previous lives, would be a far better way to go forward, to a permanent solution for many of our deepest problems.

This type of treatment is costly and time-consuming, so the normal stop-gap solution is an electric shock or packet of drugs for a quick fix and temporary relief. As usual with cutting corners, it all comes down to what we want and what we spend our resources on. Strange as it might appear to an outsider, we always have the fear-raisers with us needing money for weapons. If anybody wished to bring us down, they would not need weapons to do it. We do it very easily ourselves.

Chapter Seven

To profoundly love another, it is necessary first to learn to truly love and forgive ourselves for all our human frailties.

For a long time now, the planet has been subject to greed on a massive scale. The majority of both men and women have become blind. They have lost their way, often forgetting what they wished to be incarnated for.

All humans come into this dimension to develop their soul, to love, nurture and learn from each other, sometimes just to spend time being and not doing. Alas, many think it was for more power, money and shopping and then they wonder why they feel cheated, empty, unloved, needy and unsatisfied. For them, life is a constant search for ultimate fulfilment, the ultimate kick.

Perhaps the whole of life is just a projected dream of ours. It's inside us not outside of us and soon we will wake up. Remember how you wake from a dream or nightmare. It is very real for a time. Waking up from life is the same.

Regardless of the pattern of continuous disasters that we have all suffered under the rulership of men, worldwide there have been very few women at the helm. Those women who have recently been in power are usually but a poor and embarrassing imitation of the alpha male. One can only imagine that is what they think we want or perhaps they are the default ones that rise to power in what is basically a male world.

The time has come for the pendulum to swing to the female energy in all of us whatever our sex. The time for cooperation is upon us. So, rather than yet another helping of the over-masculine fearful competitive stance, this poor world desperately needs a balance—not destructive polarisation yet again and again.

We all of us need to take our blinkers off and these are female ones as well as male ones. Look around and really closely observe everything about you. Mention to many of the people in your life that the world is rather out of balance regarding the male and female energy input. The response will all too often be rapid and unquestioning: *'It's always been like that. Can't change it'*. You may get an uncomfortable look as if to say, *'Oh God, not one of those women's lib females'*.

As women, we just ask that we are equal. We want equal recognition, not a dole-out of concessions at the male pleasure. We don't want favours. Women have had the vote for one hundred years now but that is just a sham. We are still waiting for equal conditions and pay plus acceptance in many occupations.

Look around at your female friends as well as the male ones and you will see the unquestioning acceptance of the daily casual misogyny displayed by both sexes. Women often express this in terms of judgement of other women of how they dress, do their hair and what size their body is. They are unaware that they are aping the male in cutting women down, judging them.

Only judge the action but not the person. This attitude is ingrained throughout the world and it's about time women sat up and took notice of their judgement as well as the men's and question it. By complying and going with the flow unthinkingly just for a quiet life is living in a falsehood of acceptance. Women too are complicit in the creation of the present imbalance.

If we were to remove our fixed ideas of what is and what is not, then change our competitive stance, we could go forward in a balanced way. We can still utilise both the male as well as the female energy to have time enough to secure the future of this world and be able to actively help in its development into a more caring place for the earth and its inhabitants, be they male or female humans, animals, fish or plants. My guides tell me that both sexes are different sides of the same coin. We have the same value. So, stop jockeying for position. It wastes both time and energy.

In past civilisations, there are records of many caring and gifted female rulers. They arrived in various parts of the world when the civilised West was in a very primitive state.

There was one woman in the Tang dynasty who ruled China with great skill and wisdom even though we see her as ruthless and she would be by our standards. At the time from 655-705 B.C. all things were in clear view. It is only now that our leaders hide the nasty side of ruling.

Her name was Wu Zetian. In her reign, there was no famine because she encouraged the building of the largest and driest rice silos ever built and they are still there. The peasants' religion was Buddhism so she built for them the tallest temple in the world plus temples throughout the land to keep them contented. Her tallest temple still stands and to this day it is often repaired. She cared for her people as a mother would and with her protection they flourished. She cut the army and increased agriculture.

Traders of the world travelled to her courts because she protected the routes and did not waste resources making war with her neighbours. Under her reign, men and women from all walks of life had equal rights. Women were elected into her parliament and held the post of prime minister as well as the men. She cut a swathe through the traditional bureaucracy. The women did not ride side-saddle on horseback but wore trousers and rode astride. They were free to choose their own life partners.

Wu Zetian was not perfect. As humans, we never are. After her death, powerful men tried to obliterate all signs of her by smashing and burying the carved stone records of her reign, defaming her and pushing her into obscurity. Though not renowned for being perfect it was a far different time and place. Life was cruel then. After her death, her successor rapidly started making wars yet again.

What happened and how did the later submission of the Chinese woman come about? How did they get to wear such ridiculous constricting clothes, bind and cripple their feet, give up their equality and be subservient to the male? Complying with this behaviour was bizarre but they did it.

Another female who came to power and did good for her country but was swept away after her death was the female pharaoh who ruled Egypt around 1600 B.C. She was a first-born. Her name was Hatshepsut. She ruled for 20 years, bringing peace and prosperity. Hatshepsut's rule was spent developing trade routes. She was a pioneer, opening the sea routes and building and restoring temples and monuments for her people. What is a little sad, though, is that she often asked that her statues depict her as a man as this helped her to be accepted as a pharaoh.

After her death, the pharaoh Thutmose III took her place. His immediate contribution to the country's well-being were campaigns against both Syria and Palestine. Also, he built a temple that stood next to and completely overshadowed hers. He defaced or erased her inscriptions, records and statues. That says it all and shows fear. It appears that male rulers assert their power by scenting all perimeters like a dog. These actions are to display strength and power but the best way to be seen as powerful is to show lack of fear and display all the elements of trust and love. It takes a big person to do that.

Thank goodness we now have many female archaeologists and researchers who are righting the wrongs of the buried women of history from all things as well as all parts of the world. They are coming forward with a continuous drip of water on sandstone.

Since the ancient earth goddesses and throughout world history we have had female rulers all over the world, not all good, but the continuous rise of overwhelming male energy dominance has brought us to a situation wildly out of control and balance that needs to be centred yet again. What is the problem? Why all the effort to obliterate records of peace, prosperity and loving female rulers? Is it because it makes a country look weak?

The sad thing is that we are so often subjected to male rule and when women take their rightful place they all too often feel the need to act like men.

Women are not weak. They do not need to be anything but women, equal just the other side of the coin. They don't have to prove anything about how tough they are by annexing others' territory.

The examples of Wu Zetian and Hatshepsut are just a couple of the women from history who particularly stand out. The list is considerable and it's in many other occupations as well as ruler.

To remove ourselves from extreme swings of the pendulum, take your energy higher up the rod. The higher we ascend our thought, the higher goes the world's energy. The pendulum has swung too far towards the male energy and only now is it beginning to right itself. It must never go to such an extreme swing in either direction again.

Chapter Eight

It takes a very brave person to be transparent and honest but it leaves the soul and spirit full of light.

ANOTHER area for woman to be brushed under the carpet was in the Christian church. It started with the notorious treatment of the universally known Mary Magdalene, the close companion of Jesus. They were always together until his death. She was one of the foremost apostles and a teacher of the others.

Women were there from the start financially as well as physically, supporting and playing a large part in spreading the teachings of Jesus. On their constant pilgrimage, they were accompanied by a large following of men as well as women. They were needed to help provisioning and money-raising.

Women were with Jesus for most his teaching life. Many of the female disciples names are now coming to light. They were removed with a large chunk of the bible at the same time. Their writings were highly edited or names changed by the early Christian church, a church which did not exist when Jesus was alive and a travelling teacher. The idea of Jesus having twelve male apostles was added after his death. It represented the twelve tribes of Israel.

There are paintings of early Christian women dressed and officiating as bishops in the fourth century. There are also churches dedicated to them and their healing work. At least half of the early followers were female.

It is interesting that the church is involved with buildings, possessions and money. Jesus and his followers were travelling teachers. They did not want buildings. They had no sexual divisions in their tasks. The followers of Jesus went out to practice, heal and preach in male/female couples. It was not customary to be alone with members of the opposite sex or when working with the sick so a male/female couple could work with anyone.

Much of the education and early training of Jesus was with the Essenes. They were a peaceful community consisting of men and women both as students and teachers. Many of the early Roman converts to what came to be called Christianity attended hidden meetings held in the catacombs under Rome. These meeting places still carry defaced wall paintings depicting female teachers conducting services dressed as high ranking members of the clergy. They met in the catacombs because they needed to be careful as followers of the preacher Jesus, who was still not accepted.

Emperor Constantine was baptised as a Christian on his deathbed, bringing general acceptance of the rapidly expanding religion. Christianity, a spin-off of the Jewish belief system, was amalgamated with the religious beliefs of both the Romans and the Greeks.

Some time later, Emperor Theodosius I saw how the religion was taking hold of the population, so the new Christian church with its female side removed or debased was to become a suitable religion for the army. The army at that time was stretched around Europe. It was made up of fighting men drawn from many countries. This army needed a strong religion to unite it into a cohesive unit that would help knit together the rapidly crumbling empire with its many different belief systems. It was deliberately reformed into a male religion that was deemed more suitable for a strong male army.

The original Roman as well as the other religious beliefs were rapidly swallowed up into a religion that had removed the female in any significant equal form for the first time. The earth mother goddess of the time was turned to Mary mother of the Christ who, in turn, was turned into a deity.

God became male, the source of all things but why not an amalgam of god and goddess? God has no sex. It is a creative force, the Source of all things and of equal male and female value.

Before the Romans took over and changed Christianity, as it was to be called, a lot of the martyrs that were killed in the Colosseum games as sport were early Christian women. There is now a cross there to commemorate this. What was it that made the early church so fearful of women being equal to men as spiritual teachers? Up until then, religion for the Romans was the calling of both sexes.

With the foundation of the proselytising Christian church, a rapid campaign was undertaken to rename many of the female disciples by jettisoning them and turning their names into the male form. What we now call the bible was restructured and female writings torn out but those entrusted with this task did not destroy them as asked. They buried them in various parts of the Middle East. Large sections of the original work are being assembled again but, as usual when truth comes out of hiding, it brings fear of change with it.

The Greeks had a formalised system of gods and goddesses that were closely aligned with mother nature, the earth and the seasons of the year. These beliefs were taken on board by the Romans who gave many Roman names to them. They then merged into beliefs from the Jewish faith that went on to become modern Christianity.

Source or God as many people believe did not give us the ten commandments. The Romans did. They came from their already established culture and local law. Source does not give us commands or punishment but only love and care. We are the ones to see and make the world as rewards and punishments. The Christian belief came about and was to have its roots firmly set in an amalgam of misogynistic cultures.

The Christian church as we now know it bears hardly any relation to the teachings of Jesus. He was Jewish and was a wandering teacher and healer with no church buildings. His male and female followers were also wandering teachers. He held women in high regard.

As was customary at that time with the majority of Jewish men, Jesus had a wife who was probably the closest companion that he spent his life with. The Romans did not acknowledged her as his wife. She was called a whore and they turned the whole thing into an all-male group with him as a semi-deity. The recorders of history are rarely to be trusted. It is almost always turned to the advantage of the victor.

We were told that women were at the root of all troubles, unclean and the gateway to hell, that they must cover themselves and submit to the rule and the rather doubtful wisdom of the male. We don't know for sure when sex was aligned with wickedness, or when the great god Pan was turned into the devil, poor thing.

All that the people wished for was a bit of sexual fun, procreation and music, not continuous war with its companions of famine, death and misery. But that is all they ever get and all they will get until they, i.e. the general run of humanity, remove the blinkers from their eyes and look at and question everything.

Chapter Nine

*Religion in the past has not done us many favours.
It has been used as a tool of repression, helping to control
the people, keeping them in a place of fear and oppression.
It is divisive and is still at the root of most disputes and wars.*

As my guides advise me, avoid politics and religion. They have no relevance to life. They divide, so don't follow these things too closely as they enslave and disempower us.

One only has to look at the majority of wars today to realise that they are still based on differences of religious belief or culture. Humanity is still preoccupied with religious belief that is imposed upon them in one way or another. All religions are divisive and man-made. They are to separate them and us and our direct link to Source—dualism yet again.

The innate spirituality of all human beings has no need for state-imposed religion. That is merely another system of control. We are quite capable of thinking and deciding for ourselves. Our moral structure of control and spirituality comes from within. This cannot be imposed upon us from another being. It is innate. We are born with it. Its strength or weakness comes from our earthly development in our many previous incarnations.

Do not revere, worship or bow down to anything or anyone. It disempowers you. You give away your own power to whatever and whoever you bow down to. We are all a fractal of Source.

We have no exact idea when the automatic repression of the female—its other name is '*misogyny*'- developed in the advanced cultures of many parts of the earth. The norm in many primitive beliefs is that all power was equally balanced between the male and female. They are two sides of a never-ending turning coin. Call it what you wish but it is always of equal value. Each side is a combination of different energies, just male and female.

It is we who perceive a separation between the divine male and divine female. Always together they make one. It is not a popular view to hold but I feel that women must shoulder the blame equally with men for the continuation and acceptance of discrimination and misogyny. If women reject the advances of the misogynistic males and bring up their sons to be enlightened men, misogynistic males would always miss out and either change their ways or become extinct.

Many women have low self-esteem in a world dominated men. They appear to be grateful for any recognition and can become enamoured of any male, grateful for any male that turns up. This leads to both the man and the woman being deprived of the fulfilling relationship the soul desires.

They will have a lifetime of constantly repressing their true nature by remaining in a position of neediness. The male and female are not just attracted to each other because of sexual reasons. They are searching for their own opposite sex in this dimension. On the other side, we are a perfect balance of both sexes.

Needy searching people have often gone to the extremes of whatever sex they arrived here in, never learning to develop both sides of their emotional needs. A balance of both the male and female side of each of us is important before we can balance out with one of the opposite sex. We feel in need of this when in our body on earth but we are complete both male and female as one on our soul level.

There is no need to be sparring on each side of the boxing ring, no need to be full of fear of lack of love and abandonment. Link lightly. Don't clutch.

It is better to have mutual respect and complete confidence in one's own worth. This way, fear will not stalk the relationship. This way, too, it will not leave one in a place of need if the other wants to leave the relationship. They can continue to develop independently. Male and female must learn how all humans need a lot of love and support.

Male bullying at home and school starts from an early age to produce the conformist male. He hopes to come up scratch whatever he is thinking deep inside. Boys are told to to grow up and man up as they are pushed to the extremes of *'manly'* behaviour. Many are suppressing their needs and get a sense of low-worth, fearful of appearing as soft.

Thank god for the truly open ones that are appearing in our midst now who say what they want and need. They know it's only ego that's dented if they are rebuffed and that's negligible. The soul can see ego but ego can't see the soul. Ego is of the body, so is something to put in its place. Don't let it dominate your life. You are in charge. You are driving not ego.

What is needed between all humans as well as between us and animals is recognition and acceptance of our natural equality, whatever our differences. That way, we will feel emotionally safe with each other. Emotional safety, love and truth is all that we require in abundance. It's just down to fear and ego getting its oar in yet again. Try never to dominate either a human or an animal.

Achieving the desired outcome of natural equality will take time. We certainly have had many centuries and not got very far. Alas, we cannot continue looking the other way for what we imagine is going to be a quiet life. This is not our only life, so make this world the world you wish to return to next time around. My guides tell me that the pendulum of the male/female energy of the world has swung to the extreme of the male and desperately needs to be brought back into balance.

We all have a duty to humanity and the planet to adjust the balance of power and to stop the constant round of wars and killing. Men are by nature fantasists and are able to distance themselves from the reality of what they are doing in war. All this reflects in the irresponsible cult of war games and other fantasy video games that appeal to this characteristic. These games have an undue influence on what is expected as the behavioural norm by males.

Why are there no war memorials acknowledging the dead women, children and old persons who are the victims of war? There always have been and still are very many more of these killed than soldiers.

Now war is waged long distance by drones. This appeals to the fantasy side. It is becoming more frequent for soldiers of both sexes never to see their victims. If they did, they just might think again about directing their missiles at women, the old and children. All this is cowardly but they are given medals and pensions.

We have very few leaders now who stand up for peace and prosperity, for care and love of the earth. Never let the thought leave your mind that the other side *'your enemy'* is exactly the same as you: brainwashed. You are all equal in the eyes of Source, of God. God has no religious or political views or preferences. Only humans are dualist and humans will fight over the difference between two currents. It's pathetic. The world is a very small planet.

We all are connected. If you do not feel that, remove your blindfold and connect with your higher self as it is aware of all things even if you wish to bury your head in the sand.

Chapter Ten

*We create all of the suffering in this dimension.
We have created this world by our thoughts and actions.
Each person can change them and the world if they wish to.*

WE don't notice all the bizarre things that are the norm and are around us every day. If you were to imagine that you came on a visit from another planet, you would question why a large part of the human race complies with the wishes and religious laws of the other half. It really is very strange that the dominant side in almost every religion just happens to be male.

Rules are set by men for women to obey. Cover your head. Uncover your head. Never wear trousers. Never wear a skirt. Walk freely and be part of society. Never go out of the house without a male relative. This and very much more is still a very real life in many parts of the world today. For instance, you can still be killed if your dowry is not sufficient in some countries. It is still looked upon as looking for rape if you return home late and alone, i.e. you are asking for it.

Such men that make these laws are so often unable to control their own undisciplined behaviour. They are the ones who should be confined indoors with their eyes averted to give us all a bit of peace and safety to get on with our lives. Are we all completely mesmerised, mad or just blinkered by inertia? If it doesn't affect us personally, and even if it does, we don't query it. Yet again, it's a case of *'They should do something about it'*.

A lot of men, however civilised they might be and whatever their jobs are, clearly don't wish to upset the status quo as it was and is in many households across the world. It's great to have a little woman out at work and earning but is she still running the house and doing most of the housework? it might be a hackneyed statement but many women still scrub the lavatory in joint working households.

Think of the woman's lot just a short while ago. Housework was heavy labour and only suitable for the strength of a man. Also, in the past women were pregnant for most of their life span. In farming and then with the industrial revolution, they worked outside the house as well as birthing and bringing up children. As a matter of course, men wanted dinner in a clean house, children in bed and a compliant bed-warmer: nobody queried this expectation?

> Even now, in this world every day, women are gang-raped, killed or sexually mutilated to hold up the honour of their family, men or tribe.

> Even now, 84 per cent of Egyptian girls undergo genital mutilation and this did not happen in Egyptian past history when women had power and status.

> Even now, it is still not permissible for females to be educated in many parts of the world where it is deemed to be inappropriate and to cause trouble.

> Even now, in parts of the world, pregnant women are imprisoned, sexually tortured and both they and their unborn babies killed by men, for no reason other than the fact that they are female and *'belonged'* to men from a different region or religion.

Why do so many good enlightened men turn away and let others do this? Why do they keep such a low profile and try to run with the herd? Why are they not up in arms about this? It is something worth standing up for!

I heard a story from a friend. Although very kind, obviously she was one of those people who had not suffered sexual abuse in childhood. She laughed as she told the tale of some very funny young male working associates who showed much delight in terrorising a young female trainee.

They took their delight in goosing her for fun every time they passed her. She was upset and obviously very disturbed by them. It had never crossed their male minds that she might have suffered from childhood sexual behaviour that had traumatised her. She needed gently caring for on the sexual front as such souls often carry the scars throughout their lives, unable to pluck up the courage to communicate their feelings to another.

I have heard the jesting statement *'Don't be a silly girl'* many times from women who have not lived through such traumatisation. Sexual abuse often shows itself in both sexes, young men and women. Both can suffer abuse that is carried out by members of both sexes. Their behaviour can be very defensive or a distinct nervousness in regard to predatory sexual teasing.

We are all human and must be aware and develop our compassion, supporting all women or men that we find in this type of situation. It is not funny. We can't just *'Get over it'*. Females as well as males can display distinctly misogynistic behaviour by not questioning their own attitudes and using the patronising statement of *'silly girl'* towards a grown young woman.

Many may find the statistics of childhood sexual abuse hard to comprehend until they stop and think that every male or female that abuses a small girl or boy may well turn into future abusers and also probably has or will do this to others. They may well be the same men or women that sexually intimidate women or men in the work situation. They can easily pick up on those that are easily intimidated. They can sense it. Never forget that they are predators.

The general male population, however honourable and civilised they might be in private, when in male company like to keep a low profile or a united front, all chaps together. Sorry, that's cowardice. It's flock-of-sheep behaviour.

The time has come for all to take a stand and take responsibility for getting the male house in order. Watch what you do. Every small action helps. Don't join the flock. That is how all persecutions start, by not being active, by turning the other way.

We are manipulated each day both by our *'can't-be-arsed'* and *'it's-not-affecting-me'* attitude. Be very careful. All things are about you. Society pushes us further into a place of opposites for commercial reasons: sex sells. They use the neediness to sell anything to us—in fact, almost everything. To need something or someone is a feeling of lack. Only when we learn to love ourselves are we free to love another.

Time and time again it has been said by many that men took away women's freedom. This can't be wholly true. Women must have had a role in this. Women must have submitted.

Chapter Eleven

We are already enlightened. Allow the light through.
Clear and align the etheric bodies each day and it will have space to spread.

WE have the capabilities to make changes. There is nothing so set in its way that it can resist when the intention is powerful and true. All that is necessary is commitment to persistent resistance.

Using unity and peace is the way to walk forward with an unwavering belief of a positive outcome. Holding back and thinking or saying it would be good if this was so but *'the world is not like that, get real'* will instantly evaporate the idea, knocking the wind out of the intention. Listen to the powerful response of your heart not others' negative voices.

Concentrate on what you are for not what you are against as negative emotions are out of alignment.

The spiritual teacher Wayne Dyer's statement is oh so true: *'You will see it when you believe it'*. It's a bit of an old-fashioned sentiment but what is needed is called love and faith. Just add a powerful, unaggressive intention and persistence. Gently but firmly resisting is all that is necessary.

We already have the ingredients for a positive outcome. We made the world develop in this way. We can change it for the better. Each of us can do big things in a small way. Just believe. That will be a good start.

We do not need the doubters. They are full of fear and fear is infectious. To fear something is to put your intention towards it. Our power of intention is the most powerful gift that we have. Project it towards the dark and it gives the dark the energy to develop. We all have a choice in life. Choose to project it towards the light, towards what you are for not what you are against or fear. Negative emotions put us out of alignment.

Perhaps our expectations restrain us because expectations hold attachments on the outcome and that is a form of pre-judgement. Our expectations form our reality and we make our world from our thoughts and expectations. Expect nothing but trouble and you will get nothing but trouble.

Women in the past in many places had equality with men. It is not a new idea. In twelfth century Europe there were the Cathar women. They had equality in their finances and in the church hierarchy. They taught side by side with men.

History has put the Cathars down as joyless, religious fanatics but think of who wrote this history, the Roman Catholic church that was afraid of them and persecuted them. Fanatic is not the word to describe either them or their teaching. These people had great love and compassion. They wished to educate, enlighten and spread their love and knowledge to all from whatever walk of life.

The Cathars were highly skilled in medicine, music and the training of artisans. Their religion was one of the few to truly follow the teachings of Jesus, wishing only to teach love and for equality for all whether they be the rich landowners or poor peasants, male or female.

The Cathars owed allegiance to no-one and no dues were owed to the Roman church. This belief was to bring fear to the church, thereby causing a violent wave of repression and the mass murder of thousands of good, law-abiding people from all backgrounds across a wide swathe of Europe where they had practiced under many names.

The church whipped up fear with its hysterical accusations of heresy, the latter sentiment being rather odd as the Cathar teachings were closer to the Essenes and earlier disciples of Jesus than the Roman church ever was.

The early church was set up as a system of control and repression through instilling the fear of hell and damnation. There is no hell and never was. It's all propaganda that was used to control the population by using fear. Also, the selling of indulgences, i.e. passes to heaven, as well as tithes paid to the local abbey helped to fatten the coffers in Rome, making the church more powerful than the state.

The Roman church did not need or want a sect of self-ruled Christians who desired and lived the simple life free of a repressive central hierarchy or the corrupt priesthood that would not fill their coffers. The Cathars needed no church, fear, repression, statuary, idolatry or any of the glitzy trappings. Any place under any tree or in a friend's house was suitable for their meetings, discussions and teachings. They had no need of anyone to intercede between them and their maker.

The religion of the Roman church, with its fear of hell, did not impress them as their belief was based on the thought that hell was in this world and that they were living in it each day. The practice of being a wandering teacher bringing enlightenment, love and education to all played a major part in their way of life and system of belief.

Before the rise of formalised religion and its divisions came about, the only things that were acknowledged, celebrated and given thanks for, were the seasons and bounty of the natural world, what we now call Gaia. This sentiment was and is still acknowledged in the furthest corners of the world. The planet nurtures us. It is simple recognition and thanks for the amazing symbiosis that effortlessly runs our life.

Our bodies, never mind our surroundings, are almost too overwhelming to contemplate. The acknowledgement and thanks to nature has no label. We are all free humans.

Chapter Twelve

Light is greater than dark and will always overcome it but the dark that often looks fearful also looks enticing. We are free to choose.

LIFE for early humans was borderline survival, with the constant stress of hunger and fear of wild animal attacks. When women were in a vulnerable situation having babies, they needed protection, food and shelter to survive and secure the future of the human race.

It was convenient for populating the world for nature to have bonding in many of its creatures. Bonding between the human sexes inevitably came about and was the best solution for the security and development of humans. Much later on in our development, domination by one sex appeared to take over. This behaviour appeared to come from fear and control.

Given the almost insurmountable problems we have with the rapidly approaching planetary survival crisis brought on partially by us, not an asteroid this time, things can and must move forward in a positive direction. With this domination of one sex by another, it can be exposed for what it is: fear.

It can only be to our advantage in these times to have balance. The cooperation of all human beings is essential and we must not still be fighting on every level only to be found whistling whilst Rome burns. We may find the planet under our feet destroyed in a very short time by lack of co-operation and world unity. We do all live on it.

One step in a positive direction that can be taken to overcome our primitive fears is to try not always to separate ourselves from others who might be different from us. Try to develop our more empathetic side. Try to see our similarities and our mutual enhancement in others, not our differences. We all have something positive to contribute. Otherwise, we all will be as a bus falling over the parapet whilst the passengers are arguing over the destination.

The future of this planet lies in all our hands but particularly those of the parents of both the male and female future generations, teaching all the children to be curious and not to discriminate or encourage war or gender difference. This teaching must be undertaken by both sexes from birth and constantly reinforced because of the negative bombardment from society and its continuous stoking the fear of *'Them or That'*.

When governments stoke up fear of *'Them or That'*, it is to remove the general population's eyes from what its own bungling shortcomings are. It's one of the oldest tricks in the book and the general population falls for it over and over again.

We are no longer controlled by the church, with its threats of hell if you did not conform. The control now is hidden under the umbrella threat of imminent war, bombs, terrorists, viruses, immigrants, poverty, asteroids, global flooding and alien invasion. This last one I love, being that we are mostly all aliens to this planet.

We are an experiment and I feel the planet will be better off without us. Has it ever occurred to you that the planet lives a symbiotic existence with itself? Then we came along, homo sapiens, the superior dominator.

So the end result of all this fear-raising junk that is pumped out to us twenty-four hours a day via television, films, newspapers and video games is a paralysing fear that both shackles and disempowers us. Take time out to live without the news in any form. Only then will you wake up to the pattern of control by fear that lurks underneath everything.

Fear sells. Fear is everywhere. Fear of wrinkles sells face cream. Fear of grey hair sells hair dye. Fear of looking old sells. Fear of germs sells drainer cleaner. Oh, the things in the drain will kill you.

What is amazing is that even with all that deliberate fear flashed about is that half the population eats food that is unfit for human consumption. It is so mucked about with and filled with chemicals but the public is not made fearful as eating this food makes a profit for the food industry.

We have a natural craving for sugar and salt because they are not always available in the natural world, so food manufactures add them to food. They pad it out with wheat that turns into sugar in the body. They add very low-grade fats to everything we eat. We become addicted to this processed food and we become sick. Our bodies are made for real food, live food. Each mouthful should taste of life and love.

Perhaps it's time that we all grew up and decided to be in charge of ourselves and our own thoughts, no longer to be swept this way and that by the media and the all-consuming fear machine that is at its base, just there to generate money. We are rather like white mice in a cage bred to jump in response to commands. Do your own research and do not rely on what others tell you.

The majority of people in the so-called civilised West spend very little time discovering who they are on the soul level and what they would like to develop on this short trip. They are preoccupied with the body, which is just the vehicle, and lose touch with the essential self and its journey in this dimension.

We are primarily residing on this planet to expand, develop and experience love, joy and forgiveness in all its forms. We are not here to control or be controlled by others or by our own highly contrived fears. Remember that we are our own scenario director. Take charge.

Ego is afraid of us. It knows nothing. Ego cannot hear spirit. Ego speaks from the part of the brain that guards us from danger. It is outside of Source. So, step back. Breathe deeply. Enlighten yourself. Evolve. As you remember to breathe deeply, it will release the blocks of fear. It's not easy to be fearful when breathing deeply. Don't be engulfed by the self-manifested, horror-movie, fear-machine that you imagine is going to gobble you up in a net of terror.

Alas, many think life was for more power, shopping and money. They then wonder why they feel cheated, empty, unloved, needy and unsatisfied, For them, life is a constant search for ultimate fulfilment.

The more you give to the world, the happier and more fulfilled you become. It is not about money. It consists of what you have developed that can contribute to humanity in general. It's all about completing the circle. You were given a life; what you have taken out, give back with abundance.

Our thoughts make our reality so make a place in your life for something to be and see it there now. There is only the now. Don't try too hard. Place the seed of desire and wonder how it will come about in a positive way. Then stand back. Leave a space for your spiritual guides to manoeuvre. All will get there. Don't clutch the wheel. Don't push too hard or you might get the wrong thing.

Perhaps the whole of life is just a projected dream of ours. It's inside us not outside of us and soon we will wake up. Remember how you wake from a dream or nightmare that is very real for a time. Waking up from life is the same each time we rise to the surface. Take a breath then dive in again and again and again.

Chapter Thirteen

*Just wonder. Have no attachment to the outcome.
Surrender and flow. Believe in the now.*

IF the human being is basically just a series of algorithms that has collected information for Source from the start of creation, it is no longer efficient because the computer has a far larger and more logical brain. The only difference is that we arrive connected to our soul and all its wisdom. Our human body is part of our learning equipment and our physical inherited genes all make a big difference in how we react in this dimension.

The majority of the human race appears at this time to be unable to hold the thought of self-preservation and make sure that their world is in good enough order to enable their continuous development. The world is the base for their future spiritual expansion but it is now being consumed as seed corn. Using the old analogy, we are sitting on the branch that we are cutting off. Human beings are destroying the world that they need for their development and survival.

What is the more important: the experience of the divine intelligence that absorbs all information of the human experience here via spirit, or the survival of the human species that is after all just another animal living on this planet at this time? Even though it is used as a vehicle for spirit, humans have turned out to be unaware that they are rapidly making their planet uninhabitable. This is not the first time this has happened in thousands of universes.

The alternative is to reincarnate on our returns into an intelligence that only requires computer hosts that are good at providing a suitable environment for their work. At the moment, we are human computers that don't pay attention to our planet host.

I for one love my human body and planet earth but we are an experiment, one of many. Unless we develop, we are heading towards failure but perhaps there is no such thing as failure, just development and change. For an experiment, one releases judgment of the probable outcome. Perhaps the computers will adapt and take over as the vehicle that experiences all the human emotions. Failure can only be seen when there is an expectation of a particular outcome. We are only an experiment and there is no reason why any particular outcome should be preordained.

After all, not all planets are as beautiful as ours or have human beings occupying them. The freedom that we have here can also contribute toward our demise. Our universe contains planets that have lost their atmosphere and their inhabitants. Before we join them in their demise, it would be a great achievement for humanity with all its potential to join together, to develop, to change our ways, to go forward, to cherish our beautiful selves and our beautiful planet.

The longer humans accept greed and fear and hatred of others because of race or sex or worldly possessions, the shorter the time this planet will continue to exist. We have no real idea what is around the next corner.

I was curious as to the future relationship between our spiritual connection and the future of AI (Artificial Intelligence) that is already like a seeping flood and rising up to our ankles whilst our attention has been elsewhere. One day, I put in a request for a meeting with my guides. I needed more information. They pointed out the obvious. Where did I think information for the sudden scientific surges now or in the past comes from? It comes from Source.

We are the experiment and a new inspiration is tossed into our play pen from time to time to see what we will make of it. We have a choice to use it for the dark side or the light side.

Thoughts and words make our reality, so create what you wish to see in the world. Resist the negative or dark side through unity and peace. This is the way forward. Will we find it? I hope so, for there is far more light than dark.

Do not put your thoughts on what you do not want. Put them on what you want on the earth and what way you want the planet to develop.

Just wonder. Have no attachment to the outcome. Surrender and flow. Believe in the now. Borders between all things or people are irrelevant. Violence only attracts violence. Human consciousness is a collective of fear.

Our body comes from and is nurtured by this physical world. When we depart, we leave it behind to regenerate the planet. The body is a temporary vehicle for the spirit to manifest its desires and develop whilst on its visit in this dimension.

The world is a living energy and far more powerful than we can even contemplate. It is in control of itself and its future and has its own scenario. We are just the equivalent of water on its back. All it needs to get rid of us is to shake and it has done that many times before.

We certainly can all do our bit towards halting global warming but need to understand that the power of our thought is far greater than any action that we can take. So we must concentrate our thought on the light and the positive outcome not the dark that is just a black hole of negativity. Never give it your energy as that is thought out of alignment.

When you think ill of someone or something, that makes a thought out of alignment and thoughts that are no longer in alignment bring unhappiness and a sense of loss to the one that is thinking so.

There is no way that we can arrogantly say that there is no god. The very word god is a misnomer. It might apply to Zeus, Thor, or Mercury. All were worshipped as gods. The word god represents the energy of Source, the root of all things, the power of creation and the manifestation of love.

We are a manifestation of that continuous energy and intent.

This energy cannot vanish. It comes into this dimension and moves on from it. As we too are energy, we cannot die. That's an impossibility. We are part of the Source energy in its continuous seeking of knowledge and transformation. To die is to transcend time.

There are those who seek to understand and acknowledge the workings of Source, i.e. energy, and the total connectability of all things. That includes the innate manifesting ability available to all humanity. We might be referred to as the true, enlightened sorcerers.

Enlightened sorcery is the constant search for knowledge, delving deep into the source of all. As with all other things in this dimension, knowledge and names can be used for the positive or for the negative, for fear and the dark or for joy and the light. It's our choice. We are responsible for our choices and which direction we face.

We will repeat our mistakes of judgement until we get it right and we move on. There is no punishment other than what we deem it to be. There is only love in all its manifestations.

To remove ourselves from the extreme of the pendulum swing, take your energy higher up the rod. The higher we ascend our thought, the higher goes the world's energy.

Combining our human power of positive intention has a far greater effect on the future of the planet than we realise. Intentions are far more powerful than any physical action we may take to rebalance nature or humanity. Combine these intentions with the immeasurably greater intelligence of Gaia. Gaia will know what it wants to do.

www.ingramcontent.com/pod-product-compliance
Lightning Source LLC
Chambersburg PA
CBHW071757080526
44588CB00013B/2271